FIANCÉ VISA GUIDE FOR VIRGINIA RESIDENTS

WHAT EVERY VIRGINIA RESIDENT NEEDS TO KNOW BEFORE APPLYING FOR A FIANCÉ VISA

Fiancé Visa Guide for Virginia Residents

What Every Virginia Resident Needs to Know Before Applying for a Fiancé Visa

Kimberley Schaefer
Attorney at Law

http://ImmigrationVirginia.com

Fiancé Visa Guide for Virginia Residents

What Every Virginia Resident Needs to Know Before Applying for a Fiancé Visa

by KIMBERLEY SCHAEFER

ISBN 978-0-9837391-3-5

Published by:
Maiesta Books
http://www.MaiestaBooks.com

Disclaimer

The Publisher and the Author make no representation or warranties with respect to the accuracy or completeness of the contents of this work and specifically disclaim all warranties, including without limitation warranties of fitness for a particular purpose. No warranty may be created or extended by sales or promotional materials. Although every effort was made to ensure that the information contained herein was accurate at the time of publication, immigration law is constantly changing and the accuracy of the information contained herein may be affected by changes in immigration law. The information contained herein may not be suitable for every situation and is not legal advice specific to your situation.

If you need legal advice for your fiancé visa or other immigration case, you should seek the services of an immigration lawyer. This book, even if received from Kimberley Schaefer or Schaefer Immigration, does not create an attorney client relationship between you and Schaefer Immigration. Only a client representation agreement signed by both you and Kimberley Schaefer will create an attorney client relationship.

Books By Kimberley Schaefer

Adjustment of Status / Green Card Guide
for Virginia Residents
AdjustmentOfStatusBook.com

Do I Need an Immigration Lawyer?
ImmigrationLawyerBook.com

Family Immigration Guide
for Virginia Residents
FamilyImmigrationBook.com

Fiancé Visa Guide
for Virginia Residents
FianceVisaBook.com

Immigrant Visa Guide
for Virginia Residents
ImmigrantVisaBook.com

Immigration Mistakes You Can't Afford To Make
ImmigrationMistakesBook.com

Immigration Waiver Guide
for Virginia Residents
ImmigrationWaiverBook.com

Marriage Immigration Guide
for Virginia Residents
MarriageGreenCardBook.com

Introduction

Thank you for your interest in this book.

This book is for you if you are interested in learning more about the fiancé visa process. If you are reading this, you probably just got engaged or are considering getting engaged. This is likely one of the most exciting times of your life.

Don't let immigration issues add stress to this exciting time in your life. This book provides you with an overview of the fiancé visa process so that you can better understand what is involved in getting a fiancé visa. Also included is a list of the information you'll need to collect to begin the process as well as a discussion of whether you need an immigration lawyer to help you.

To be fair, I should point out that this book doesn't try to cover everything. This book does not attempt to cover every detail of the fiancé visa process. It also does not attempt to explain to you how to fill in each blank on the forms that are completed as part of the fiancé visa process. That information is simply beyond the scope of this book because the answers will depend on your specific circumstances.

If you have decided to work with a lawyer to get your fiancé visa, then you should read the section on finding the best immigration lawyer for your case before you hire a lawyer. As that section points out, your goal should be to find the best immigration lawyer for your case. Depending on your situation, I may not be the best lawyer for you. But my hope is that this book will help you get in contact with the best immigration lawyer for your case.

If you have any questions about the fiancé visa process and how you can work with me to get your fiancé visa, please feel free to contact me at:

contact@ImmigrationVirginia.com

Office: (703) 424-2979
Toll free: (877) 887-9523

Schaefer Immigration
1818 Library Street, Suite 500
Reston, VA 20190

Notes On Terms Used In This Book

You'll notice that I use the term fiancé throughout this book. As you probably already know, the dictionary defines fiancé and fiancée as:

> *Fiancé refers to a man who is engaged to be married.*
>
> *Fiancée refers to a woman who is engaged to be married.*

From the immigration law point of view, it doesn't matter if you are applying for a visa for your fiancé or your fiancée. To simplify things, I simply use fiancé in this book. It is just too awkward to use either "fiancé(e)" or "fiancé or fiancée" everywhere.

I also use the generic terms "immigration officer" or "officer" throughout this book. Depending on the context, this could be a USCIS immigration officer, a Department of State consular officer at an embassy or consulate overseas or a Customs and Border Protection officer at a port of entry. For readability purposes, I use "immigration officer" or "officer" for whichever government employee is in a position to make a decision on your immigration case.

Finally, you may be familiar with the term "K1 visa" which is just another term used for a fiancé visa. I use fiancé visa in this book instead of K1 visa because I find that it reads better.

Table of Contents

Fiancé Visa Overview

Fiancé Visa Qualifications

Not everyone will qualify for a fiancé visa. Some of the initial requirements that you should consider include:

- Only United States citizens can file a petition for a fiancé visa. If you are a permanent resident, you should consider other marriage based immigration options or wait until you become a citizen before starting the fiancé visa process.

- You must demonstrate your relationship to your fiancé and your intent to marry each other for the purpose of having a joint life together.

- You and your fiancé must be eligible to marry. This means that if either of you have been married in the past, you will need to be able to show that your previous marriage has ended.

- You must show that you have met at least once in person in the last two years, or you must qualify for an exception to this requirement.

- Your foreign fiancé must not be "inadmissible" to the United States, or you will need to qualify for a waiver. The grounds of inadmissibility are complicated and include such things as criminal convictions, misrepresentations on past immigration applications and previous immigration violations.

- You must marry within 90 days of the date your fiancé enters the United States.

The above list does not include everything that needs to be considered. If you work with an immigration lawyer, your lawyer will carefully review your situation to verify that you meet all of the requirements. If you don't meet the fiancé visa requirements, your immigration lawyer will be able to assist you in developing an immigration strategy that will help you and your fiancé begin your life together in the United States as quickly as possible.

If you decide to apply for a fiancé visa without the assistance of an immigration lawyer, you should carefully review all of the requirements before you submit any forms to the government. ***You should not rush to submit your forms.*** It will take time to learn the details of the fiancé visa process, but this will be time well spent. After all, submitting your package if you don't meet all of the requirements or without the supporting evidence needed to win your case will result in significant delays, added expenses, and possibly a visa denial.

Take the time to learn as much as possible about the fiancé visa process before you begin. This includes doing legal research to understand why other people have had their applications denied so that you don't make the same mistakes. If you don't have the time or research resources to do this, you should try to work with an immigration lawyer.

Fiancé Visa Application Process

There are two basic steps to applying for a fiancé visa:

STEP 1: FIANCÉ VISA PETITION

The fiancé visa petition process begins when a United States citizen submits a Form I-129F petition on behalf of their fiancé. The I-129F is also called the fiancé visa petition. This petition requests that your fiancé be allowed to enter the United States so that you can get married. You will need to wait for your petition to be approved before you can move on to the consular processing stage.

STEP 2: CONSULAR PROCESSING

The consular processing stage begins after the fiancé visa petition is approved and the petition package is forwarded to the National Visa Center. The package will stay at the National Visa Center for a short time before being forwarded on to the embassy.

The embassy will contact you with information on how to schedule your fiancé visa interview. During this stage you will need to submit the fiancé visa application along with the supporting documents such as a medical exam report and police certificates.

Assuming that all goes well at the interview, your fiancé will be issued a fiancé visa and will be able to join you in the United States so that you can get married.

There is a final step that is not part of the actual fiancé visa process, but that is very important. It involves the application to get a green card after you get married:

STEP 3: ADJUSTMENT OF STATUS / GREEN CARD APPLICATION

After you get married, your new spouse will need to submit an application for what is called "adjustment of status". This is the process that allows your spouse to get permanent resident status and a green card. After your spouse submits the adjustment of status application, a green card interview will normally be scheduled. If all goes well at the interview, your spouse will get a green card in the mail shortly after the interview. If you have been married less than two years, the green card will be a "conditional green card" which means that in two years you'll need to file a separate application to remove the conditions on the green card.

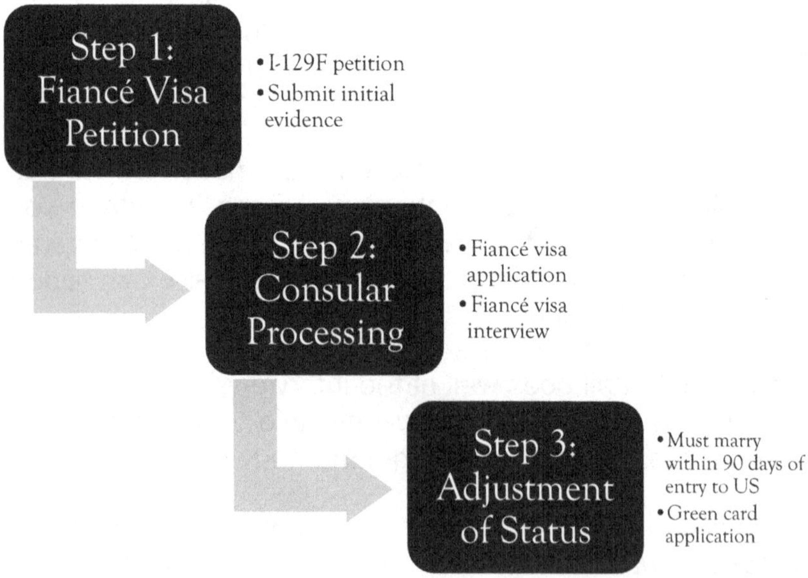

How Much Does It Cost To Get A Fiancé Visa?

The total costs for the entire process, including the green card application process, will typically range from $2,000 to $5,000. These costs are broken down into three categories: government fees, other required costs and legal fees.

Government Fiancé Visa Fees

$340 Form I-129F filing fee

$240 K-1 visa fee

$1,070 Form I-485 adjustment of status fee

Other Required Costs

Medical exam – changes by doctor and location

Passport photographs – changes by photographer

Translation costs – varies by the translator and type of documents being translated

Original documents/certified copies – varies by case

Legal Fees

The legal fees for a fiancé visa case will vary by law firm and the complexity of the case. If you decide to work with an immigration lawyer, you should focus on finding the best immigration lawyer for your case. Later in this book, I discuss how to find the best lawyer for your case.

How Long Does It Take To Get A Fiancé Visa?

The expected waiting time for approval of an I-129F fiancé visa petition is five months. Some petitions will be approved more quickly and others may take more time.

After your petition is approved, the package will be forwarded on to the embassy or consulate near your fiancé. The length of time for an interview to be scheduled will depend on which embassy or consulate will conduct the interview. Some locations have a large backlog and it will take longer to receive an appointment at those locations.

Overall, you should expect that it will take at least six to eight months before your fiancé receives a fiancé visa, and it would not be unusual for it to take closer to one year. The wait could be considerably longer if you receive a request for evidence or you have difficulty in obtaining the required documents. Working with an immigration lawyer can help you to minimize any delays in your case.

The Fiancé Visa Interview

Many people view the fiancé visa interview as the most intimidating part of the fiancé visa process. After all, the ability to live happily ever after in the United States with your chosen partner is at stake!

After preparing and submitting all of the required fiancé visa paperwork, your fiancé will be scheduled for an interview at a nearby United States embassy or consulate.

This interview is very important and successfully passing the fiancé visa interview is a requirement in order to get a fiancé visa.

The following tips should help you with your preparation for your fiancé visa interview:

- Every embassy or consulate has its own procedures. Because of this, it is very important to be flexible and to follow the guidance that you receive from your local United States embassy. Don't rely on unofficial information that you find on the Internet, as it may be outdated or be specific to a different embassy.

- Every interviewing officer will have his or her own way of doing the interview. Be flexible during the interview and adapt to the interviewer's way of conducting the interview.

- Check with the embassy ahead of time to see what you can bring to your interview. In particular, you should verify whether you are allowed to bring electronic devices such as cell phones with you. In addition, if you have young children, you should verify if they need to accompany you to the interview.

- If your United States citizen partner wants to attend the fiancé visa interview with you, you should verify before your scheduled interview that they'll be allowed into the embassy with you.

- Your fiancé visa interview can be as short as a couple of minutes. Due to the heavy work loads of embassy personnel, your interview normally will not last more than 30 minutes to one hour. Be mindful of the time constraints of your interviewer by being prepared with your documents and providing focused answers to the questions you are asked.

- Your fiancé visa interview may be at a walk up window, not in an office setting. Depending on the security measures at the embassy, you may end up conducting your interview through a bullet proof window. Don't let the informality of this setting fool you into not taking the interview seriously.

- Be prepared to be at the embassy for some time as you may end up waiting for your interview. Do your best to be patient while you wait. Acting impatient will not help you get your fiancé visa any faster.

- Be prepared at your fiancé visa interview with copies of everything that was previously submitted as well as any additional evidence you want to submit to show your relationship. Also pay close attention to any instructions that tell you what original or certified copies you need to bring to the interview. The interviewing officer won't be able to approve your case if you don't bring the required documents to the interview.

- Don't be surprised if you don't receive your visa immediately after the fiancé visa interview. It is fairly common for the embassy to keep your passport and to return it to you a couple of days later with your visa stamp inside.

- The interviewing officer's job during the interview is to decide whether you qualify for a fiancé visa. Your job during the interview is to demonstrate to the interviewer that you do qualify. Keep in mind that the burden is on you to prove that you qualify for a fiancé visa, the burden isn't on the interviewing officer to prove that you don't qualify for one. With this in mind, you should provide honest and complete answers to the questions you are asked. Providing vague, incomplete, or evasive answers will not help you in proving your case to the interviewer.

Questions and Answers

What Happens After Your Fiancé Arrives In The United States?

You and your fiancé must marry within 90 days. It is very important that you marry within 90 days of your fiancé's entry into the United States. If you do not, your fiancé may enter into an unlawful immigration status and there may not be any way to get your fiancé back into a lawful immigration status.

After you marry, your fiancé can apply for adjustment of status and become a permanent resident. After being a permanent resident for three years, your fiancé may then be eligible to submit a naturalization application to become a United States citizen.

It is very important to review the qualifications for citizenship before submitting a naturalization application. If you submit a naturalization application when you don't qualify for citizenship, you risk losing your application fee and possibly being deported.

Does my fiancé need to apply for a green card in addition to a fiancé visa?

Your fiancé will not automatically become a lawful permanent resident and get a green card when you get married. After you get married, your new spouse will need to file a Form I-485 along with all of the required supporting documents in order to get a green card.

I have a criminal conviction, can I still petition for my fiancé?

In many cases, a criminal conviction will not prevent you from being able to petition for your fiancé. However, there are certain types of criminal convictions that could limit your ability to obtain a fiancé visa for your partner. You should discuss any criminal convictions that you may have with your immigration lawyer to make sure that you won't run into problems with the fiancé visa process.

How much money do I need to make to be eligible to sponsor my fiancé for a fiancé visa?

The income requirement for sponsoring someone for a fiancé visa is 100 percent of the federal poverty income guideline. For the adjustment of status application for your new spouse to get a green card, most people must show that they meet the income requirement of 125 percent of the federal poverty income guideline.

The following numbers should give you an idea of what the federal poverty income guideline means:

Sponsor's Household Size	100% Poverty Guideline for 2011	125% Poverty Guideline for 2011
2	$14,710	$18,387
3	$18,530	$23,162
4	$22,350	$27,937
5	$26,170	$32,712

Your immigration lawyer will be able to help you determine the correct number for your household size based on your situation. In addition, if you don't think that you will meet these income requirements, you should discuss this topic with your immigration lawyer. You may be able to meet the income requirement by showing assets or by getting a joint sponsor.

What are the reasons that fiancé visas are denied?

At the initial stage of the fiancé visa petition, common problems include not completing the forms completely, not including all of the required initial evidence, and not meeting the basic eligibility requirements.

However, even if the fiancé visa petition is approved, that does not guarantee that the fiancé visa will be approved during the interview at the embassy. One of the most common reasons that fiancé visas are denied during the interview stage is because the person conducting the interview is not convinced that the relationship is bona fide.

This often happens when only the bare minimum of supporting documents are submitted. You should keep in mind that it is your job to demonstrate to the officer conducting the interview that your relationship is real. You should make sure that you submit evidence that is well-organized and that clearly demonstrates that you plan to have a joint life together and meet all of the requirements for a fiancé visa.

One of the roles of an immigration lawyer in the fiancé visa process is to help you identify the evidence that will best demonstrate to the interviewing officer that you qualify for a fiancé visa. Your immigration lawyer will also help organize your supporting documents so that it is easy for the officer conducting the interview to see that your fiancé visa should be approved.

What if we don't marry within 90 days of my fiancé entering the United States?

You are required to get married within 90 days of your fiancé entering the United States. If you get married after 90 days, you should immediately discuss your situation with an immigration lawyer so that you can identify the best strategy for helping your new spouse get a green card.

What if my fiancé doesn't marry me after coming to the United States on a fiancé visa?

If your fiancé enters the United States using a fiancé visa and then doesn't marry you or marries someone, then they will not be able to file an adjustment of status application from within the United States. They would need to instead consider whether an immigrant visa and consular processing is an option. If this situation applies to your case, you should discuss your options with an immigration lawyer.

My fiancé was denied a tourist visa in the past. Is a fiancé visa still an option?

Depending on why the tourist visa was denied in the past, a fiancé visa may still an option. But, if your fiancé has ever been denied for any sort of visa in the past, you should bring this to the attention of your immigration lawyer.

One of the key issues that your immigration lawyer will want to explore is the reason for the past denial. If there was any sort of fraud or misrepresentation with the prior visa application, your immigration lawyer will need to know about it in order to evaluate whether an immigration waiver will be needed for a fiancé visa.

You should let your immigration lawyer know if you previously followed the advice of an "immigration consultant" who claimed that the only way to get a tourist visa was to say that you were married when you really were not. This type of misstatement may be viewed as a misrepresentation which would require an immigration waiver. If this applies to your situation, you should work with your immigration lawyer to develop a strategy to overcome this problem. In addition, you will need to be prepared to prove that you weren't married even though you said you were on your previous tourist visa application. *I strongly advise you against trying to resolve this type of misrepresentation issue without the assistance of an immigration lawyer.*

In addition, if there have been several visa applications that have been denied in the past, your immigration lawyer will likely want to work with you to present a very strong case for your fiancé visa application. This is because it may appear to the immigration officer conducting the fiancé visa interview that your fiancé is simply looking for any way to get to the United States and is now trying a fiancé visa application since the other visa applications didn't work. The best way to overcome this mindset is to present strong evidence of your relationship with your initial fiancé visa petition.

Can we just get married using a tourist visa?

If your fiancé entered the United States using a tourist visa, you should not try to file an adjustment of status application to get your new spouse a green card while they are still in the United States without first discussing your case in detail with an immigration lawyer. **Depending on the specific facts of your case, it could be viewed as visa fraud if the government believes that your spouse entered the United States on a non-immigrant tourist visa when the real intent was to get married and remain in the United States as an immigrant.** If you know that you plan to get married, you should apply for a fiancé visa and not take the risk of being accused of visa fraud because you used a tourist visa to get married and apply for a green card.

Can my fiancé visit while we wait for the fiancé visa?

If your fiancé has a tourist visa, it may be possible for your fiancé to visit the United States while you are waiting for the fiancé visa interview. However, you will need to make sure that your fiancé returns home for the fiancé visa interview and does not violate any of the terms of the tourist visa.

If your fiancé tries to enter the United States on a tourist visa after the fiancé visa petition has been filed, your fiancé should be prepared to show the immigration officer at the border or airport evidence that the trip really is just a short trip and that the intent is to return home to complete the fiancé visa process. If the immigration officer is not convinced that the trip is only going to be for a short visit, your fiancé may not be allowed to enter the United States.

My fiancé has a criminal conviction. Is a fiancé visa still an option?

It will depend on the type of criminal conviction. Although some types of criminal convictions will not be a problem with the fiancé visa process, other types of criminal convictions will make your fiancé inadmissible to the United States. This means that your fiancé will not be able to get a visa and will not be able to enter the United States unless your fiancé is able to get an immigration waiver to overcome the criminal conviction.

The issue of the immigration consequences of criminal convictions is very complex. If your fiancé has a criminal conviction, you should get copies of all of the police reports and court records related to the conviction so that your immigration lawyer can review them. It is very important for your lawyer to review the actual police records and court documents, because those are the documents that the government will review when deciding whether your fiancé needs a waiver and is eligible for one.

NOTE: You should keep in mind that immigration law has a very broad definition of the term "conviction". *Many alternative sentencing programs or expunged convictions may still be considered to be a conviction under immigration law.* You should discuss any arrest with your immigration lawyer as early as possible in the fiancé visa process.

Is it possible to get a fiancé visa if we haven't met in the last two years?

Although there are limited exceptions to the requirement that you have met your fiancé in person within the last two years, it can be very difficult to qualify for one of these exceptions. If it is not possible for you to travel to your fiancé's country to meet, you should consider whether there is another country that both of you could travel to in order to meet in person.

If you believe that there is no way for you to personally meet with your fiancé, you should discuss this issue with your immigration lawyer.

I don't have copies of my tax returns. What other options do I have for showing the required financial support for my fiancé?

You can obtain information on how to request copies of your official IRS tax transcripts by visiting:

ImmigrationVirginia.com/request-irs-tax-transcripts/

In addition to getting copies of your IRS tax transcripts, you should also try to get an employment verification letter from your employer, three months of pay stubs and copies of your bank statements. Your immigration lawyer will be able to advise you on which documents should be submitted based on your particular situation.

Where can my fiancé get the required medical exam?

Each embassy will designate one or more local doctors who can perform the required medical exam. It is very important that you get your medical exam done by one of the approved doctors because medical exams done by other doctors will not be accepted. The embassy that will be doing your fiancé visa interview will give you a list of the approved doctors for your medical exam.

If you do not complete the vaccination supplement as part of your initial medical exam as part of the fiancé visa process, you may need to get the vaccination supplement completed as part of filing the adjustment of status package to get your green card after you get married. You can locate a doctor who can do this for you at:

ImmigrationVirginia.com/find-uscis-approved-doctor/

Fiancé Visa Checklist

Collecting the information about yourself and your fiancé is one of the first things that you'll have to do as part of the fiancé visa process. Although the checklist in this book doesn't cover everything that could come up in preparing the fiancé visa petition and visa application, it does provide a good starting point for collecting the information needed for your I-129F petition.

Information About You (the United States Citizen Petitioner)

Supporting Documents

- Legal documents showing that all previous marriages have been terminated (such as divorce decrees or death certificates)
- Birth certificate
- Naturalization certificate (if any)
- Certificate of citizenship (if any)
- Copies of all pages of passport (if any)
- One passport style photograph

- Copies of legal documents that show any legal name changes (such as marriage certificates, adoption decrees or court orders)

Other Information

- Full name
- Current address
- Place of birth
- Date of birth
- Other names used (including maiden name)
- Social Security number
- A number (if any)
- Have you ever filed a visa petition for someone? If yes, please provide details.
- For each residence over the last five years:
  - Full address
  - Date residence started
  - Date residence ended
- For last address outside the United States of more than one year:
  - Full address
  - Date residence started

  - Date residence ended
- For each employer over the last five years:
  - Name and address of employer
  - Occupation
  - Date employment began
  - Date employment ended
- Last occupation abroad that you worked at (if any)
- For each prior spouse:
  - Full name
  - Date of birth
  - Date and place of marriage
  - Date and place marriage ended
- For petitioner's mother:
  - Full name (including maiden name)
  - Date of birth
  - Place of birth
  - City and country of residence
- For your father:
  - Full name

  - Date of birth
  - Place of birth
  - City and country of residence

- How was your citizenship acquired? (birth in the U.S., naturalization, parents)
- If naturalized, provide number of naturalization certificate, date and place it was issued
- If you have ever obtained a certificate of citizenship, provide certificate number, date and place issued
- Do you have any criminal convictions?

Information About Your Fiancé

Supporting Documents

- Legal documents showing that all previous marriages have been terminated (such as divorce decrees)
- Birth certificate
- Copies of all pages of passport
- One passport style photograph
- Copies of legal documents that show any legal name changes (such as marriage certificates, adoption decrees or court orders)

Other Information

- Full name
- Current address
- Intended address in United States
- Place of birth
- Date of birth
- Country of citizenship
- Other names used (including maiden name)
- Social Security number (if any)
- A number (if any)
- Have you ever been in the United States? If yes, please list for each visit your immigration status (student/visitor/etc.) and the dates you arrived and departed.
- Has anyone ever filed a visa petition on your behalf? If yes, please provide details.
- For each child:
    - Full name
    - Date of birth
    - Country and city of birth
    - Present address

- For each residence since age 16:
  - Full address
  - Date residence started
  - Date residence ended
- For last address outside the United States of more than one year:
  - Full address
  - Date residence started
  - Date residence ended
- For each employer over the last ten years:
  - Name and address of employer
  - Occupation
  - Date employment began
  - Date employment ended
- Last occupation abroad that you worked at (if any)
- For each educational institution attended:
  - Name and address of school
  - Starting date (month/year)
  - Ending date (month/year)
  - Course of study and degree or diploma awarded

- Have you ever served in the military? If yes, please provide:
    - Branch of military service
    - Rank or position and military specialty
    - Dates of service
- For each prior spouse:
    - Full name
    - Date of birth
    - Date and place of marriage
    - Date and place marriage ended
- For your mother:
    - Full name (including maiden name)
    - Date of birth
    - Place of birth
    - Current address
- For your father
    - Full name
    - Date of birth
    - Place of birth
    - Current address

Additional Documents and Information

The USCIS filing fee for the Form I-129F petition is $340, payable by check or money order made out to "U.S. Department of Homeland Security".

You will also need to submit copies of any documents or other evidence showing your relationship and that you have met in person at least once in the last two years. This can include travel documents, photographs, letters, emails, Internet chat transcripts, phone records, etc. Your immigration lawyer will work with you to identify whether there are other documents that should be included in your package.

You should also include a description of how you met, how your relationship developed and the time you have spent together. You should discuss any specific wedding plans that you have made.

If you are related to your fiancé, you may need to include information on the nature and degree of your relationship (e.g. third cousin, maternal uncle, etc.)

Do I Need An Immigration Lawyer To Help Me Get A Fiancé Visa?

There is no requirement to use the services of an immigration lawyer in order to get a fiancé visa. But, many people will find the services of an immigration lawyer to be extremely valuable to successfully navigating the fiancé visa process.

What An Immigration Lawyer Can Do For You

You should not hire an immigration lawyer to simply fill out forms for you. Although your immigration lawyer will normally prepare any required forms, this is not their primary role. Your immigration lawyer's main responsibilities are to provide you with sound legal advice, identify legal issues, research and draft legal briefs (if needed for your case), communicate with government officials on your behalf and represent you at immigration interviews or hearings.

An experienced immigration lawyer can:

- ✓ Help minimize the time you are separated from your fiancé by providing you with legal advice on your options to reunite as quickly as possible
- ✓ Help you to avoid unnecessary delays by keeping your case on track

- ✓ Help you get your application approved quickly by ensuring that your application is submitted correctly and with all of the necessary evidence
- ✓ Save you the stress of dealing with USCIS and the Department of State by communicating with them on your behalf
- ✓ Represent you if the government requests additional information about your case
- ✓ Represent you if you need to file an appeal in the event your application is denied
- ✓ Provide legal advice and assistance if you need to apply for a waiver

In addition, your immigration lawyer will typically help you by:

Verifying that you meet all the requirements before you submit your application.

In some cases, it may not be clear if you meet all of the requirements for a fiancé visa or adjustment of status. If you don't qualify, your application will be denied, and your filing fee will not be refunded. Because the nonrefundable filing fees for immigration applications can cost hundreds – if not thousands – of dollars, your lawyer will help you verify that you meet the basic eligibility requirements before you pay the filing fee.

Identifying and evaluating all of your possible immigration options.

Your immigration lawyer will help you identify each immigration option that may allow you to achieve your goals. Depending on your situation, you may have more than one option that you could pursue. You may have better options than a fiancé visa. Your lawyer will help you determine which option would be the best for you.

Evaluating whether any criminal convictions will cause problems with the fiancé visa process.

Many criminal convictions (even misdemeanors) can create serious immigration consequences. Again, if you have **any type** of criminal conviction – even if the conviction was expunged or you were given an alternative sentencing or diversion program – you should let your immigration lawyer know about it. Your lawyer will likely want to review the criminal court records to identify what immigration consequences you may face and if there is any way to minimize or eliminate those consequences. Keep in mind that marriage to a United States citizen does not necessarily overcome immigration problems caused by criminal convictions.

Assisting you with preparing and filing your fiancé visa petition, fiancé visa application and adjustment of status application.

Your immigration lawyer will also assist you with preparing and filing your fiancé visa petition, fiancé visa application and adjustment of status application. This will include the correct completion of all of the necessary forms, as well as presenting the necessary supporting evidence in a way that will make it easier for the immigration officer who reviews the package to see that your application should be approved.

How To Find An Immigration Lawyer For Your Fiancé Visa Case

Choosing a lawyer to represent you is obviously an important decision. The task of choosing the right immigration lawyer for your fiancé visa case is complicated by the fact that there are many areas of immigration law. Some lawyers specialize in business or employment immigration issues, while others focus on cases involving litigation, such as immigration court hearings or immigration appeals.

For your fiancé visa case, you'll want to make sure that you focus your search for a lawyer on those immigration lawyers who accept fiancé visa cases. If an immigration waiver may be needed for your case, you should also make sure that your lawyer accepts cases involving waivers (not all lawyers accept waiver cases). So, how do you know which lawyer to choose for your immigration case? A good starting point in hiring an immigration lawyer is to check whether the lawyer accepts cases like yours.

The decision of which lawyer to hire should certainly not be made on the basis of advertising alone. *The Yellow Pages* and Craigslist are filled with ads – all of which say basically the same thing. You should not hire based solely on advertising. Instead, you should hire the lawyer that you trust to do the best job on your case. You shouldn't even hire me unless you trust that I can do a good job for you.

You also cannot rely solely on the recommendations of friends and family. The fact that a lawyer did a good job on a friend's DWI case or a relative's divorce does not make him or her the best attorney for your fiancé visa case. Immigration law is very complex. Just because a lawyer is very skilled in another area of law, that does not mean she will be able to effectively handle the legal matters of your fiancé visa case. Likewise, just because a lawyer did a good job with your friend's employment-based immigration case, that does not mean she will be the best choice for your fiancé visa case. I cannot stress it enough: Immigration matters are different and difficult, and they require an attorney who is skilled and specifically familiar with immigration law.

I also caution you to avoid relying solely on "directories" of lawyers, especially those claiming to list the "best" or "top" lawyers or those that provide lawyer rankings. The determining factors for where lawyers fall on this list can be very skewed. If the directory doesn't tell you exactly how they select the "best" lawyers or how they rank them, how do you know the rankings reflect what is important to your case? After all, is a lawyer the "best" simply because they paid to be included in the directory? Is it really important how many academic articles a lawyer has published? Are you looking for an academic writer, or an attorney who can successfully prepare and present your fiancé visa case? You should be careful to avoid blindly relying on the rankings supplied by other people unless you know that those rankings reflect what is important to you.

This does not mean you should altogether ignore directory listings or referral services. Rather, I caution you to be wary of relying on rankings provided by others unless the person doing the ranking can describe how they came up with the rankings and you are confident that the rankings reflect the factors that are important and relevant to you and your case. General directory services can be a useful tool in helping you locate immigration lawyers in your area that you may want to add to your initial list of lawyers to contact. You should also add to your list the lawyers who are recommended to you by friends and family and the lawyers you identify through your own research, including Internet searches.

Which Immigration Lawyer Is Best for You?

How do you find out which lawyer is the best in your area for your fiancé visa case? I believe there are key questions you should ask. These will help you determine the best lawyer for your case. It will involve some time on your part, but that's a fair price to pay to find the best representation for your case.

The "best" immigration lawyer for you will depend on many things, including your personal preferences. Some important considerations are discussed below. These are not in any particular order because what is important to one person may not be important to another. The items discussed below, however, should give you a good starting point in deciding which immigration lawyer is best for you.

Consultation Policy

I've found that many people call my office and ask about my consultation policy before they ask about anything else. If you are choosing an immigration lawyer based on the lawyer's consultation policy, you should make sure that you understand what the lawyer means by "consultation."

For example, some lawyers offer a free phone consultation; others offer free office consultations; and still others charge a fee for consultations. The choice that each lawyer makes is based on many issues.

The most important thing to keep in mind is the purpose of the consultation. Your primary goal in a legal consultation should be to identify whether the lawyer is a good fit for you and your immigration case. You should not expect an immigration lawyer to be able to provide you with detailed legal advice during an initial consultation, especially if the consultation is short or your issues are very unique or detailed. As discussed above, immigration issues are complex. You should not be surprised if a lawyer needs to take a closer look at your case before providing you with specific legal advice.

Think of the consultation as more of a job interview: You are considering whether or not to hire that attorney. Use the consultation to decide if you would feel comfortable working with the lawyer. Also, take note of whether or not the lawyer can describe immigration options to you in a way that you can understand. In many cases, the lawyer may be able to identify the options that should be explored in your case and explain exactly how they would go about identifying the best option for you.

Willing To Provide General Information

Is the lawyer willing to provide you with some general information before you hire them? In particular, can they provide you with helpful information to help you decide whether the lawyer is a good fit? You should feel comfortable that the lawyer can and will do a good job for you, is a good personality match for you, and can and does explain things in a way that you can understand.

You should check to see if the lawyer is willing to provide you with some general information so you can get a better feel for whether the lawyer is a good fit for you in all of these important areas. If the lawyer has a website or blog, visit those websites and check them for information that may help you decide if it is the right attorney for you. Does the lawyer offer any materials (such as this book) that you can read before you hire the lawyer? Resources that will help you get a better feel for who the lawyer is?

Is the lawyer willing to explain at your initial meeting the basic issues in your case and how she would handle your case? Are they willing to tell you this even before you commit to hiring them? Keep in mind that there is a difference between providing general information and specific legal advice. It is reasonable to ask a lawyer to provide general information or to summarize the steps they would take to identify the best course of action for your case; however, you should not expect to receive legal advice specific to your situation until you have hired the lawyer and the lawyer has had the opportunity to speak with you and review your documents and evidence to learn the details of your case.

Location Of Office

Depending on your situation, the location of the lawyer's office may also be an important factor in deciding which immigration lawyer is best for you. I have offices in Reston, Virginia, Fairfax, Virginia and Washington, DC where I can meet clients.

However, I understand that for many of my clients it can be difficult to take time off from work just to meet with me. I also have clients who live outside of the Northern Virginia area. For these clients I offer to work with them using email, phone/Skype and mail. For many types of cases, such as fiancé visas, the entire case can be done without personal meetings if my clients are comfortable working with me long distance.

In addition, you should keep in mind that there are only two offices in Virginia that conduct green card interviews for the adjustment of status part of the fiancé visa process. One is located in Fairfax, Virginia and the other is in Norfolk, Virginia. If you live outside of these areas, you should consider whether you would be comfortable going to the interview on your own without your lawyer. It will be easier and more convenient and affordable for a lawyer with an office close to the USCIS office to attend your interview with you than it would be for an attorney who is based further away. You should carefully consider whether you would be comfortable working with your attorney via phone and e-mail and whether or not it would be a viable option for you to travel to their office for any meetings.

Location can also be an issue when choosing between lawyers located in your local geographic area. If you don't have access to a car, does public transportation provide convenient access to the lawyer's office? If you will only be able to take short breaks from work in order to meet with your lawyer, is the lawyer's office located close to your workplace? Is the lawyer such a good match in every other way that you don't mind having a longer drive to visit them for face-to-face meetings and discussions? These are all important questions to ask before choosing a lawyer.

Personality

It is not uncommon for immigration matters to take months or years to resolve. Bearing this in mind, you should consider whether the immigration lawyer is a good personality match for you. After all, you probably don't want to spend months or years working with someone who you simply don't like to be around!

Does the lawyer take the time to explain things in a way that you can understand?

As you probably already know, immigration law is very complex. Does the lawyer explain the issues important to your case so that you can understand them? The odds are that whatever the issue is, if it is important to your case, you'll want to understand it so that you can make the best decisions and choose the best options for you. Be sure your lawyer can effectively communicate with you.

Lawyer's fee

Most likely, the lawyer's fee will also be a factor in deciding which lawyer is the best one for you. Key items related to the lawyer's fee that you should consider are: value, affordability, and whether the lawyer accepts the form of payment you want to use, such as credit cards.

The value of a lawyer's fee should be an important consideration, but you should avoid using the lawyer's fee as your sole basis for hiring a lawyer. In other words, don't go looking for a bargain! You should not simply shop around for the lawyer with the lowest fees – you don't do that when you need another professional such as a doctor or dentist do you?

Instead, you should focus your search on finding the best immigration lawyer for your fiancé visa case:

- Are you confident in the lawyer's ability to represent you?
- What is the overall value that is being offered?
- What is included with the fee?
- Will you be charged extra for phone calls, online legal research, or postage?
- Will the lawyer attend your interview with you, or would that entail an additional fee?
- Will you be charged extra if the government requests additional information in your case?

When it comes to the fiancé visa process, you should make sure that you understand whether the quoted fee includes just the I-129F fiancé visa petition or if it also includes the additional forms needed to apply for the fiancé visa at the embassy. It is also important to know if the fee includes assistance with the adjustment of status application so that your new spouse can get a green card.

You should not assume that you cannot afford to hire an immigration lawyer to assist you with your fiancé visa case. You may be surprised to learn that hiring an immigration lawyer to assist you can be just as affordable as hiring a non-lawyer immigration consultant.

Language Barrier

Keep in mind that English is the language that will be used to communicate with USCIS. Therefore, you must hire a lawyer who can effectively communicate in English.

At the same time, you should feel comfortable in communicating with your lawyer. If your native language is not English, how important is it to you that your immigration lawyer speaks your native language? If you are not comfortable discussing your case in English and the lawyer doesn't know your native language, would you be comfortable working with a translator? Does the lawyer have someone in their office who can translate, or do you have a friend who would be willing to help? There are no right or wrong answers to these questions: The important thing is that you are comfortable working with your lawyer and that you and your attorney can find a way to effectively and clearly communicate.

Membership in Professional Organizations

Because immigration law is constantly changing, it is important that you hire an immigration lawyer who is able to keep up with the changes. One of the best ways for a lawyer to do this is to join a professional organization such as the American Immigration Lawyers Association (AILA). AILA is a national association of over 11,000 lawyers and law professors who practice and teach immigration law. Among other things, AILA provides continuing legal education and information that helps its members stay up to date with new developments in immigration law. I am a member of AILA and receive daily updates of new developments. These updates help me to ensure that my clients are not surprised by any new developments that may affect them or their cases. If your lawyer is not a member of AILA, you should ask them what steps they take to keep up to date with changes in immigration law.

About Virginia Immigration Lawyer Kimberley Schaefer

When people ask me what I do, I often tell them, "I help future Americans become citizens." After all, American citizenship is the eventual goal of almost all of my clients, and I help them achieve that goal.

I am an immigration lawyer practicing law in Virginia and Washington, DC at Schaefer Immigration. In addition to helping people in Virginia and Washington, DC, I can also help people from throughout the United States with their immigration cases.

I initially became interested in immigration law while completing intensive consular officer training offered by the Department of State at the National Foreign Affairs Training Center in Arlington, Virginia. My interest in immigration law deepened while providing consular services in Lagos, Nigeria. I have an international background and have lived or worked in the United States, Europe, Asia, and Africa.

I also believe that it is important for people to have access to good information about the immigration process when they are trying to decide what the best options are for their immigration case. My website provides helpful information to people before they complete any immigration forms or hire an immigration lawyer:

http://ImmigrationVirginia.com

In addition, my books such as *Immigration Mistakes You Can't Afford to Make* are also aimed at providing useful information to my clients.

For my clients who are outside of the Northern Virginia and Washington DC area, I work with them using a combination of phone calls/Skype, email and mail. In addition, many of my clients in the Northern Virginia area choose to work with me via phone calls/Skype, email and mail instead of meeting in person at my office. This provides them with greater flexibility on when and how we communicate and allows them to minimize the time they need to take off from work.

For clients who prefer to meet in person, my Reston, Virginia office is conveniently located at the Reston Town Center. I can also meet with clients in Fairfax, Virginia. My DC office is located across the street from the Farragut North Metro station and one block from the Farragut West Metro station, providing my clients with easy access to my office via the Orange, Blue and Red Lines. There is convenient parking in the area and several major bus lines stop within one block of my office.

I am a member of the American Immigration Lawyers Association (AILA), a national association of over 11,000 attorneys and law professors who practice and teach immigration law.

I graduated *magna cum laude* from Georgetown University Law Center and was awarded the Order of the Coif honor in recognition of graduating in the top 10 percent of my law school class. While in law school, I served as the Notes Development Editor of the *American Criminal Law Review*. Prior to attending law school, I served as a communications officer in the United States Marine Corps and worked in both the private and public sectors.

I am licensed to practice law in the District of Columbia. My practice outside the District of Columbia is limited to immigration and nationality law.

About Schaefer Immigration

The main office of Schaefer Immigration is located in Northern Virginia at the Reston Town Center. This office is conveniently located near the Reston Avenue exit on the Dulles Toll Road at:

1818 Library Street, Suite 500
Reston, VA 20190

There are several free public parking garages located at the Reston Town Center.

Additional offices are located in Fairfax, Virginia at:

3915 Old Lee Highway Suite 22-B
Fairfax, VA 22030

And in Washington, DC at:

1000 Connecticut Avenue, NW, Suite 900
Washington, DC 20036

You can contact Schaefer Immigration by phone at:

Phone: (703) 424-2979
Toll Free: (877) 887-9523

You can also email Schaefer Immigration at:

contact@ImmigrationVirginia.com

NOTES

NOTES

NOTES

Made in the USA
Monee, IL
04 November 2026

67387009R00036